Taking Off

T0012196

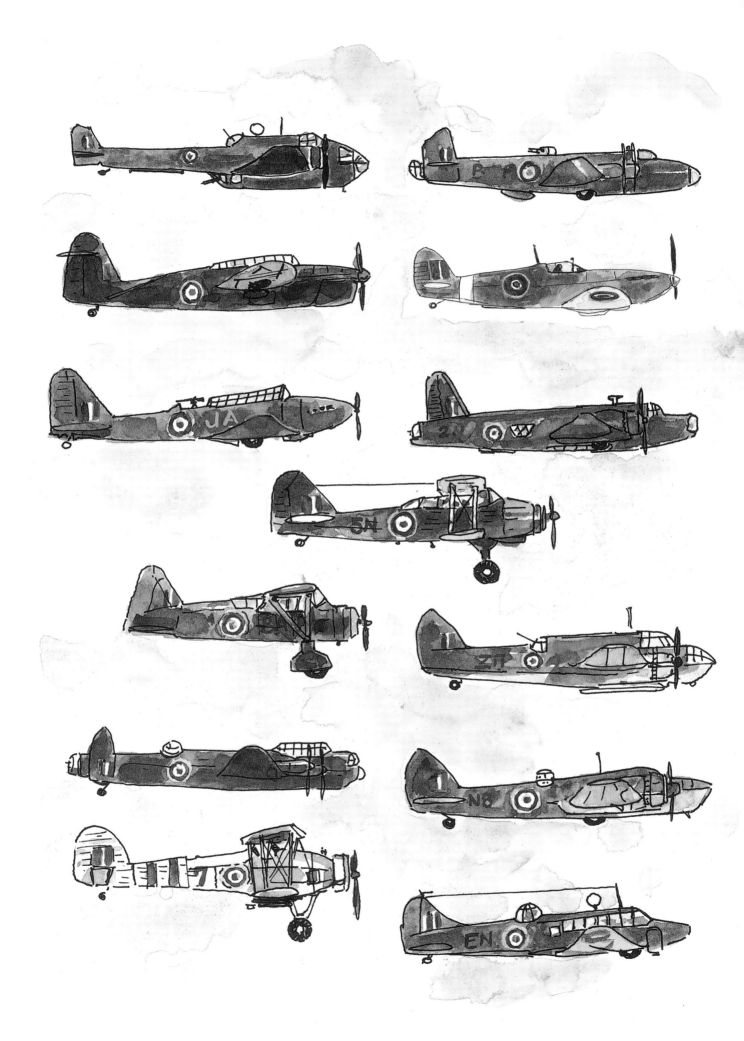

Taking Off

AIRBORNE WITH MARY WILKINS ELLIS

EMILY ARNOLD McCULLY

MARGARET FERGUSON BOOKS

HOLIDAY HOUSE · NEW YORK

FOR LIZA AND ANNIE, BOTH HIGHFLYERS

Special thanks to Maggie Simmons, who spotted a great story and sent it to me,
and to Michael Korda for sharing his encyclopedic knowledge about
planes and experiences in the the cockpits of Spitfires

Margaret Ferguson Books
Copyright © 2022 by Emily Arnold McCully
Printed and bound in September 2023 at C&C Offset, Shenzhen, China.
The artwork was created with pen and ink and watercolor on watercolor paper.
www.holidayhouse.com
First hardcover edition, 2022 • First paperback edition, 2024

3 5 7 9 10 8 6 4 2

Library of Congress Cataloging-in-Publication Data

Names: McCully, Emily Arnold, author.
Title: Taking Off: Airborne with Mary Wilkins Ellis / Emily Arnold McCully.
Description: First edition. | New York : Margaret Ferguson Books
Holiday House, [2022] | Includes bibliographical references. | Audience: Ages 6 to 8
Audience: Grades K-1 | Summary: "A biography of Mary Wilkins Ellis,
a woman pilot who flew planes for Britain's Air Transport
Auxiliary during World War II and ran an airport on the Isle of Wight" —Provided by publisher.
Identifiers: LCCN 2020055103 | ISBN 9780823449668 (hardcover)
Subjects: LCSH: Ellis, Mary, 1917-2018—Juvenile literature.
Women air pilots—Great Britain—Biography—Juvenile literature.
Air pilots, Military—Great Britain—Biography—Juvenile literature.
Spitfire (Fighter plane)—Juvenile literature. | Great Britain.
Air Transport Auxiliary—History—Juvenile literature. | World War, 1939-1945
Aerial operations, British—Juvenile literature.
World War, 1939–1945—Participation, Female—Juvenile literature.
Airplanes—Great Britain—Ferrying—History—20th century—Juvenile literature.
Classification: LCC D786 .M343 2022 | DDC 940.54/4941092 [B]—dc23
LC record available at https://lccn.loc.gov/2020055103

ISBN: 978-0-8234-4966-8 (hardcover) • ISBN: 978-0-8234-5691-8 (paperback)

$\mathcal{M}$ost winters when she was small, Mary Wilkins caught pneumonia. Watching birds from her bed, she longed to be with them in the sky.

She got her first chance in the summer of 1925, when she was eight. Cobham's Flying Circus came to the airfield in the nearby village of Brize Norton. Mary begged her father to take her. He also had a secret longing to fly, so he said yes.

Cobham's stunts made the audience gasp and cover their eyes. Mary kept hers wide open. After the show, Cobham offered rides in his deHaviland 60 Moth plane for five shillings. Pa cheerfully paid.

Mary sat on a pile of pillows so she could see over the edge of the cockpit. Cobham fired up the engine and they rose higher and higher until her parents and everything familiar—even their farm when they flew over it—was spread below like toys in a nursery. She had to have lessons!

Cobham told her she needed to wait until she was sixteen years old. She asked Pa if she could have them then. They were expensive. Given his love of flying, he quickly agreed.

Once she was old enough, Mary spent every school holiday at the airfield, mastering the skills and the calm focus and resourcefulness it takes to fly a plane. She never felt fear.

After she got her pilot's license, she enjoyed flying for pleasure for a few years, until 1939 when Adolf Hitler began to conquer Europe—first Czechoslovakia, then Poland. On September 3, Britain declared war on Germany and civilian flights were banned. Mary was grounded!

In 1940, Hitler invaded more countries, including France, just across the English Channel. In September 1940, the unthinkable happened—German pilots bombed London, and they continued to do so for the next fifty-six days.

Mary and her family listened along with the rest of England to Prime Minister Winston Churchill's stirring speeches on the radio. Churchill gave people hope and courage. Mary wanted to join the fight to defend her country, but women weren't allowed to do so. Didn't the government know that women were just as patriotic as men?

One night in September 1941, Churchill had just finished speaking when Mary heard an announcement: English factories were turning out hundreds of new kinds of warplanes to fight back against Germany. Royal Air Force (RAF) pilots couldn't be spared to transport them to military airfields across the country. The Air Transport Auxiliary, or ATA, was doing the job. Civilians, including women, with pilot's licenses were urgently needed.

Mary let out a whoop. She had a license. She could apply.

Her mother didn't want her to join the ATA. But her father said it was all right, as long as she didn't actually fight.

Mary hadn't flown in nearly two years. She was afraid she wouldn't be accepted.

The ATA examiner who interviewed Mary said she was clearly an excellent candidate, but she'd have to prove herself on a solo flight in a Tiger Moth used for training. With its wooden frame and no brakes, starter, or flaps, it was like a toy.

Mary felt nervous when she took off. It was freezing in the cockpit. But the wave of joy that always came with being aloft swept anxiety away and gave her confidence. After putting the plane through its paces, she began her descent and, as instructed, cut off the engine to simulate a forced landing. A sudden stiff wind blew the Tiger Moth violently off course. Mary managed to regain control. She kept the nose up as she glided down and rolled to a stop. It was a perfect landing.

The examiner asked if she could report the next day. Mary said she could. She took a training course and was placed in a ferry pool based in Hamble, in the south of England.

Mary's ferry pool consisted of fifteen young women, each one a passionate pilot like herself. Mary quickly made friends with Rosemary, Philippa, Vera, Doreen, Dora, and the rest.

They had to deliver more than seventy different kinds of the airplanes that were being manufactured in factories all over England, and there wasn't time to learn how to fly each kind. The women were flown in air taxis to the factories, where they were assigned planes. Before taking off, they consulted a book called *Ferry Pilot Notes* that was issued by the ATA and filled with tips and checklists contributed by other pilots. Then they flew the planes to the RAF basnd th at needed them.

Instruments and radios interfered with military communications, so they navigated with maps, a compass, their watches, or landmarks like rivers and roads. This meant they had to fly below one thousand feet so they could see the ground. The hardest part of any flight was spotting camouflaged airfields.

All the women wanted to fly Spitfires. Designed for speed, they were the fastest and most nimble of the fighter planes. But the pilots had to take whichever planes they were assigned.

Mary sometimes flew fifteen planes a day, many of which she'd never even seen before—including Hurricanes, Barracudas, Walruses, Mosquitoes, and Wellington bombers. Built for a five-man crew, the Wellington was like an airborne elephant. When Mary sat in the pilot's seat for the first time, the tail looked like it was a mile away. After landing it smoothly, she felt pretty proud of herself until the ground crew ran up looking for the pilot.

"*I'm* the pilot!" she said.

They didn't believe her and searched the plane.

In October 1942, Mary was thrilled to finally be assigned a Spitfire. She primed the engine, shouted to the ground crew to clear the propeller, and pressed the start button. The plane shuddered as the engine roared to life. Mary released the brakes and taxied to the takeoff point, then opened the throttle and the plane shot into the air. When she hit 150 miles per hour, she gave a shout of joy. It was pure freedom, and hers alone.

Bad weather was a frequent problem, but it seldom stopped the pilots from flying. Only if a church spire a mile away wasn't visible before takeoff was a flight canceled. Navigating in fog became Mary's specialty, and she earned the nickname "the fog flyer."

Once, Mary was cruising along when a plane drew up right next to her, as if trying to push her off course. The tail had a swastika, but the pilot grinned at her. Furious, she waved him away and he waved back. She refused to budge, and finally he disappeared.

There was always the chance of danger, even in fine weather. One sunny day, Mary was flying over a forest when everything went quiet. The engine had stopped. The plane was falling, but it all seemed to happen in slow motion. Was there any place to land?

She found a patch of open ground in a field and prepared for a crash landing. Mary was very frightened, but she was an excellent pilot.

She landed the plane without damaging it or herself. As she sat thanking her lucky stars, a herd of cows surrounded the plane, scaring her more than the landing had.

She was eventually rescued by a group of Royal Marines stationed nearby, who took her for tea.

Some pilots died, nearly always in accidents. Their names were erased from the assignment board the next day. When that happened, Mary swallowed hard and kept going.

Every thirteen days the women had two days off. But Mary seldom had time to go home. Once, she delivered a plane to the RAF airfield that had been built in Brize Norton, where she had taken her flying lessons. She was told her next flight was delayed.

Mary borrowed a bicycle and pedaled madly to her family's farm for a cup of tea with her delighted parents.

In 1943, Mary and Dora were ordered to deliver a pair of Spitfires to the same air base. The weather was poor, but they set off in high spirits. They were soon enveloped in thickening fog and lost sight of each other. After an hour, Mary couldn't see a thing. Her map and her watch told her she was nearing her goal.

She began her descent and finally spotted what looked like a runway. In minutes, she touched down with a thump and a giant sigh of relief.

Suddenly there was a deafening roar to her right, and another plane coming from the opposite direction streaked past on the runway, its wing tip inches from Mary's. Her heart raced.

The other plane was Dora's! She'd overshot the field and turned around. They had just avoided a head-on collision because they'd both remembered one of the most important lessons they'd learned: land to the left on the runway.

As the war dragged on, all of England seemed to be struggling. But Churchill's broadcasts continued to lift spirits. They gave Mary hope that the warplanes she delivered would bring victory someday.

And then on May 8, 1945, Mary's ferry pool heard the familiar rasp of Churchill's voice announce that the war had been won. Germany was defeated. Everyone shouted and hugged. Many fell silent, thinking of the pilots who had died in service.

Mary Wilkins had flown more than one thousand warplanes, four hundred of them Spitfires. She had always known she was born to fly. She was also born to help change history.

Because Mary had flown so many planes, she was transferred to the RAF to be a flight instructor.

After retiring, she started an air taxi company. One of her customers bought an airfield near Sandown on the Isle of Wight. He made Mary its manager.

She guided flights onto runways that were kept mowed by her little herd of sheep.
One of her hobbies was racing cars. She won many rallies in her black Allard.

Mary lived and worked at Sandown, piloting the occasional Spitfire, until she died at the age of 101, still in love with flight.

Author's Note

MARY WILKINS ELLIS was born February 2, 1917, and died July 24, 2018. Mary was one of over thirteen hundred pilots in England's Air Transport Auxiliary, 168 of whom were women. The ATA pilots delivered more than 309,000 airplanes of 147 different kinds to Royal Air Force pilots at the various airfields in Britain that were bases for the war against Nazi Germany. The ATA members joked that the letters stood for "Anything to Anywhere."

At first there was opposition to using women in the ATA. The founding editor of a British magazine, *Aeroplane*, wrote: "The menace is the woman who thinks that she ought to be flying in a high-speed bomber when she really has not the intelligence to scrub the floor of a hospital properly." The women soon proved themselves.

Planes were being turned out at a frantic pace. A single factory produced 320 Spitfires a month, and they had to be moved as quickly as possible to bases. Other planes weren't as much fun to fly. Tiger Moths had freezing open cockpits and dawdling speeds of less than 60 miles per hour. The Barracuda and Mosquito were tricky to land.

After delivering a plane, the women might be returned to their home ferry pool in an air taxi or they might have to spend the night at an air base without any facilities for their comfort.

The ATA's contribution to victory in World War II was finally recognized by the government in 2008. The prime minister awarded medals to the surviving pilots, who had been holding regular reunions over the years.

You can find lots of films, interviews, and photographs about the ATA on the Internet. Many of the women, like Mary Wilkins Ellis, published lively memoirs of their exciting experiences in the air.

For a while after the war, Mary was a flight instructor for the RAF. During that time, she was the second woman to fly Britain's first jet fighter, the Gloster Meteor, solo.

Mary Wilkins (later Ellis), circa 1941.

Next, she started an air taxi business. One of her customers bought an airfield near Sandown on the Isle of Wight and made Mary its manager, the first woman in Europe to run an airport. In 1961 she married another pilot, Don Ellis, and they lived next to the runway.

One of Mary's hobbies was car rallies. She won quite a few in her Allard sports car.

Many times during her long life, Mary was called upon to talk about her exciting work for the ATA. "Up in the air, you're on your own," she told a TV interviewer. "And you can do whatever you like. I flew four hundred Spitfires. . . . I love the Spitfire; it's everybody's favorite. I think it's a symbol of freedom. And occasionally [in later years] I would take one up and go and play with the clouds. I would like to do it all over again. There was a war on, but otherwise it was absolutely wonderful."

Source Notes

Permission to use photo of Mary Wilkins Ellis granted by Maidenhead Heritage Centre.

Pg. 18: "*I'm* the pilot!"; Pg. 23: "the fog flyer"; Pg. 36: "The menace . . . hospital properly"; "Up in the air . . . absolutely wonderful": Davison, Phil. "Mary Ellis, wartime volunteer who flew Spitfires, dies at 101." *The Washington Post*, July 28, 2018.

Additional Sources

Ellis, Mary. *A Spitfire Girl: One of the World's Greatest Female ATA Ferry Pilots Tells Her Story*, as told to Melody Foreman. Barnsley, England: Frontline Books, 2017.

Hyams, Jacky. *The Female Few: Spitfire Heroines of the Air Transport Auxiliary*. Stroud, England: History Press, 2012.

Air Transport Auxiliary Museum: atamuseum.org

First Aero Squadron Foundation: firstaerosquadron.com/2018/07/27/mary-ellis-one-of-britains-wwii-ferry-pilots-flies-into-sunset

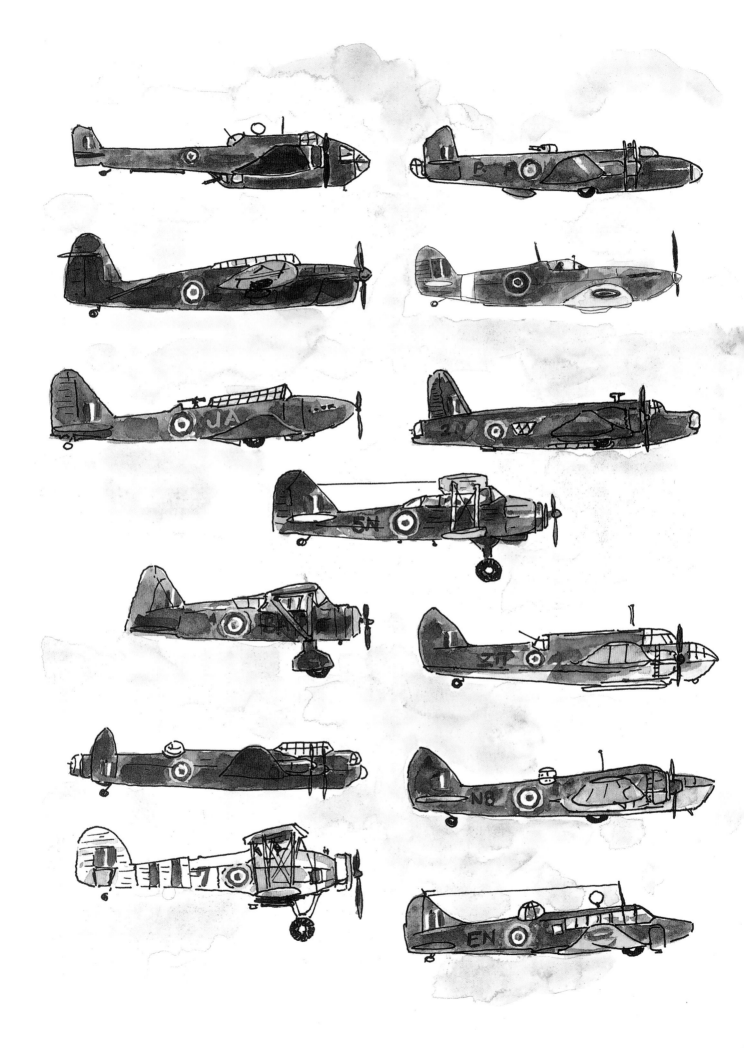

"The personality and details of Mary Wilkins Ellis's story fly off the page."
—*School Library Journal*

"This handsome picture-book biography introduces a courageous woman who followed her dream."
—*Booklist*

"McCully's ink line and watercolor artwork sports an airy translucence that invites viewers to project themselves into the skies. . . ."
—*The Bulletin of the Center for Children's Books*

EMILY ARNOLD McCULLY has illustrated many books for children including *Mirette on the High Wire*, which received a Caldecott Medal; *Dreaming in Code: Ada Byron Lovelace, Computer Pioneer;* and *Kate's Light: Kate Walker at Robbins Reef Lighthouse* by Elizabeth Spires, which received a starred review in *School Library Journal*. She lives in Austerlitz, New York. You can visit her at **emilyarnoldmccully.com**.